CW00520381

Introduction

In recent years, there has been much excitement and anticipation surrounding the concepts of 15-minute cities, central bank digital currency, and digital identities. These ideas have been presented as the solutions to some of the world's most pressing problems, promising to reduce pollution, increase efficiency, and improve financial inclusion. However, these utopian visions hide a darker side, one that is often ignored or downplayed.

In this book, I will explore the dystopian potential of 15-minute cities, central bank digital currency, and digital identities. I will examine how these concepts could be used to control people, limit their freedom, and create a surveillance state. I will present evidence and arguments that challenge the prevailing narratives about these concepts, and will encourage readers to think critically about the potential consequences of their implementation.

First, we will explore the concept of 15-minute cities. The idea behind a 15-minute city is that all the amenities and services that a person needs can be found within a 15-minute walk or bike ride from their home. This concept has been touted as a way to reduce congestion, pollution, and commuting time, while promoting community and reducing social isolation. However, the implementation of 15-minute cities could also lead to a loss of freedom of movement and a lack of variety in people's lives. In a 15-minute city, people are restricted to a small area, limiting their options and potentially leading to a lack of diversity in cultural experiences. In addition, the concept of 15-minute cities could be abused to control people, limiting their access to services and amenities based on their behavior or social status.

 Second, we will examine the concept of central bank digital currency. The idea behind this concept is to create a digital version of fiat currency that can be used for transactions. This would eliminate the need for physical cash and reduce transaction costs, while also increasing financial inclusion. However, the implementation of central bank digital currency could also lead to a loss of privacy and financial freedom. Central bank digital currency would be trackable and traceable, meaning that every financial transaction a person makes could be monitored and recorded. This would give governments unprecedented control over people's finances, potentially leading to abuse and discrimination.

Finally, we will explore the concept of digital identities. The idea behind digital identities is to create a unique, digital profile for each person that would be used to verify their identity and facilitate transactions. This would reduce fraud and increase efficiency, while also enabling greater access to services and resources. However, the implementation of digital identities could also lead to a loss of privacy and autonomy. Digital identities would be linked to a person's every move, potentially allowing for constant surveillance and control. In addition, the use of digital identities could lead to discrimination and inequality, as those without a digital identity could be excluded from participating in society.

Throughout this book, I will present evidence and arguments that challenge the prevailing narratives about 15-minute cities, central bank digital currency, and digital identities. I will encourage readers to think critically about the potential consequences of these concepts, and to consider the trade-offs between convenience and freedom. Ultimately, I hope that this book will encourage readers to question the prevailing narratives about these concepts and to consider the dystopian potential of their implementation.

Chapter 1: The Dark Side of 15-Minute Cities

The 15-minute city is an urban concept that has gained momentum in recent years as a potential solution to various urban problems such as congestion, pollution, and social isolation. The concept envisions a city where all amenities and services are located within a 15-minute walk or bike ride from a person's home. This includes schools, hospitals, parks, restaurants, grocery stores, and more. In theory, 15-minute cities can promote a sense of community, reduce commuting time, and lower carbon emissions, among other benefits. However, in practice, the implementation of 15-minute cities poses many challenges, and the potential for abuse cannot be overlooked.

One of the most significant challenges associated with 15-minute cities is the question of how to provide all necessary amenities and services within a 15-minute radius of each person's home. This requires careful planning, investment in infrastructure, and community engagement. The physical design of 15-minute cities must be carefully crafted to ensure that people have access to everything they need to lead healthy and fulfilling lives. However, even with careful planning, the potential for abuse is present, and it is crucial to identify and address such risks.

One of the most significant risks associated with 15-minute cities is the potential for discriminatory practices. In theory, the concept of 15-minute cities can promote social cohesion and inclusivity, bringing people of all backgrounds together. However, in practice, the potential for exclusion is present. One potential way that this can happen is through the selective provision of services and amenities based on income and social status. For example, affluent areas may receive better infrastructure and services than poorer neighborhoods, leaving those residents in poorer communities without access to essential amenities. This could perpetuate existing social inequalities and create further divisions within cities.

Moreover, the 15-minute city concept can be abused for purposes that are directly opposed to the interests of residents. In some cases, 15-minute cities may be implemented to control people and limit their freedom of movement. For example, if governments mandate that citizens live within 15-minute walking distance of their workplaces, schools, and medical facilities, it would limit their options for where to live. This would make it difficult for residents to express themselves freely and to participate in society as they see fit.

Another potential abuse of 15-minute cities is the potential for excessive monitoring of residents' movements. The implementation of 15-minute cities requires the development of smart infrastructure that enables the constant monitoring of residents' movements, behaviors, and activities. The data collected could be used to identify and track individuals, monitor their political affiliations, or personal habits, and potentially lead to intrusive surveillance.

The implementation of 15-minute cities could also lead to a reduction in cultural diversity within urban environments. While the concept can promote social cohesion and interaction, it may also contribute to the homogenization of urban areas. As the development of 15-minute cities requires careful planning, it could lead to a standardization of urban design and architecture, with all neighborhoods looking the same. This could have a negative impact on cultural diversity and could lead to a lack of creativity and innovation.

One of the most concerning potential abuses of 15-minute cities is the potential for exclusion of certain groups of people based on their background or lifestyle. While the concept is intended to promote inclusivity and social cohesion, it could lead to the exclusion of people who do not fit the "ideal" model of a 15-minute city resident. For example, residents who require more space, have disabilities, or work outside of the city may not be able to participate in the 15-minute city lifestyle, leading to further exclusion and marginalization.

While the 15-minute city concept has potential benefits, it is crucial to consider the potential risks associated with its implementation. The potential for abuse of the concept cannot be ignored, and it is essential to identify and address these risks before implementing 15-minute cities.

Governments must ensure that the implementation of 15-minute cities does not perpetuate existing social inequalities or create new ones. Instead, they must prioritize inclusivity and ensure that all residents, regardless of their income, social status, or background, have access to essential amenities and services. Governments must also ensure that the development of 15-minute cities does not lead to excessive monitoring or infringement on residents' privacy.

Furthermore, the design of 15-minute cities must not lead to the homogenization of urban areas. The development of such cities must prioritize the preservation of cultural diversity and the promotion of creativity and innovation.

To ensure that 15-minute cities do not lead to the exclusion of certain groups of people, governments must engage with all stakeholders, including residents, community groups, and businesses. The development of 15-minute cities must be a collaborative effort that prioritizes inclusivity and community input.

In conclusion, while the 15-minute city concept has potential benefits, the risks associated with its implementation cannot be ignored. Governments must take a cautious approach and ensure that the development of 15-minute cities promotes inclusivity, diversity, and community engagement. By doing so, 15-minute cities could become a solution to many urban problems and promote sustainable urban development.

Chapter 2: The Potential Dystopian Risks of Central Bank Digital Currency

Central Bank Digital Currency (CBDC) is a relatively new concept that has gained significant attention in recent years. CBDCs are digital currencies that are issued and backed by central banks, which could have the potential to revolutionize the global financial system. While there are potential benefits to CBDCs, such as increased efficiency and financial inclusion, there are also significant risks and potential implications that must be carefully considered. In this chapter, we will focus on the potential dystopian risks of CBDC implementation, including government surveillance, loss of privacy, and loss of financial autonomy.

Government Surveillance

One of the most significant dystopian risks of CBDC implementation is the potential for increased government surveillance. CBDCs would provide central banks with unprecedented access to individuals' financial data and transactions. This could lead to a significant loss of privacy and the potential for abuse by governments. Governments could use this information to monitor and track individuals' spending habits, political affiliations, and even their location.

Furthermore, governments could use CBDCs to impose financial sanctions or restrict access to funds for individuals who do not comply with government policies or who express dissenting views. This could lead to a significant erosion of civil liberties and a loss of financial autonomy for individuals.

Loss of Privacy

Another significant risk of CBDC implementation is the potential loss of privacy. CBDCs could provide central banks with access to individuals' financial data, which could be used to build detailed profiles of individuals' spending habits, financial history, and even their personal lives. This information could be used to target individuals with advertising, conduct credit checks, and even influence political campaigns.

The potential loss of privacy could have significant implications for the economy as a whole. Individuals may be less likely to engage in financial transactions if they are concerned about their privacy being compromised. This could lead to a significant reduction in economic activity and growth.

Loss of Financial Autonomy

The implementation of CBDCs could also lead to a significant loss of financial autonomy for individuals. Central banks would have greater control over the money supply and payment system, which could limit individuals' ability to make financial decisions that align with their personal values and goals.

For example, central banks could use CBDCs to implement negative interest rates, which would penalize individuals who save money. This could incentivize individuals to spend their money rather than save it, which could lead to a significant reduction in savings rates and long-term financial planning.

The implementation of CBDCs could lead to the consolidation of financial power in the hands of central banks and governments. This could lead to a significant reduction in the role of commercial banks and other financial institutions, which could impact their profitability and business models.

Central banks must ensure that they have appropriate legal, regulatory, and technical infrastructure in place to mitigate these risks and ensure that the benefits of CBDCs are maximized while minimizing the potential for dystopian outcomes. As CBDC issuance continues to gain momentum around the world, it will be important to closely monitor its impact on the global financial system and make any necessary adjustments to ensure its success while safeguarding civil liberties and individual autonomy.

Mitigating Risks of CBDC Implementation

While the potential dystopian risks of CBDCs are significant, there are steps that can be taken to mitigate these risks and ensure that the benefits of CBDCs are realized.

1. **Robust Privacy and Security Infrastructure**

Central banks must ensure that they have robust privacy and security infrastructure in place to protect individuals' financial data and prevent unauthorized access. This could include the use of encryption, multi-factor authentication, and secure storage of data. In addition, central banks must ensure that they have appropriate data protection laws and regulations in place to prevent the misuse of financial data.

2. **Limited Government Access to Financial Data**

Central banks must also limit government access to individuals' financial data to prevent government surveillance and abuse of power. This could be achieved by implementing strict data access controls and requiring judicial oversight for any government requests for financial data. In addition, individuals must be informed about the types of financial data that will be collected and how it will be used.

3. Protection of Financial Autonomy

Central banks must ensure that CBDCs do not infringe on individuals' financial autonomy. This could include providing individuals with options for how they use their CBDCs, such as the ability to convert CBDCs into other currencies or assets. In addition, central banks must ensure that they do not impose negative interest rates or other policies that would limit individuals' ability to save money and plan for their financial future.

4. Collaboration with the Private Sector

Finally, central banks must collaborate with the private sector to ensure that the benefits of CBDCs are maximized while minimizing the risks. This could include working with commercial banks and other financial institutions to ensure that CBDCs are interoperable with existing payment systems and can be used in a variety of financial transactions. In addition, central banks must work with fintech companies to develop innovative CBDC-based financial services that enhance financial inclusion and economic growth.

In conclusion, CBDCs have the potential to revolutionize the global financial system, but they also present significant dystopian risks that must be carefully considered. The potential for increased government surveillance, loss of privacy, and loss of financial autonomy are significant concerns that could have significant implications for civil liberties, economic activity, and the global financial system as a whole.

To mitigate these risks, central banks must ensure that they have appropriate legal, regulatory, and technical infrastructure in place to protect individuals' financial data and prevent government abuse of power. In addition, central banks must ensure that CBDCs do not infringe on individuals' financial autonomy and work with the private sector to maximize the benefits of CBDCs while minimizing the risks.

As CBDC issuance continues to gain momentum around the world, it will be important to closely monitor its impact on the global financial system and make any necessary adjustments to ensure its success while safeguarding civil liberties and individual autonomy. By carefully balancing the potential benefits and risks of CBDCs, we can ensure that they play a positive role in the global financial system and contribute to greater financial inclusion, economic growth, and prosperity.

Chapter 3: Digital Identities: The Risks and Benefits

In the digital age, digital identities have become an essential part of our daily lives. A digital identity is the set of personal data that identifies an individual in the digital world. Digital identities can be created through a wide range of means, including social media profiles, email addresses, mobile phone numbers, and other online accounts. Digital identities are used for a variety of purposes, such as accessing online services, making payments, and proving identity. While digital identities offer numerous benefits, they also pose significant risks to individual privacy and security. In this chapter, we will explore the potential negative aspects of digital identities while also considering the potential benefits.

The Risks of Digital Identities

1. Identity Theft and Fraud

One of the most significant risks associated with digital identities is identity theft and fraud. Criminals can use stolen digital identities to open fraudulent bank accounts, take out loans, or make online purchases, causing significant financial damage to individuals. Moreover, cybercriminals can use digital identities to impersonate individuals and engage in fraudulent activities, leading to reputational damage and other negative consequences.

2. Privacy Breaches

Digital identities are vulnerable to privacy breaches, which can occur when personal data is stolen or leaked. This can occur through cyber attacks or through the sale of personal data to third parties. When digital identities are breached, individuals' sensitive data, such as passwords, financial information, and personal identification documents, can be exposed, leading to identity theft and other negative consequences.

3. Infringement of Personal Freedom and Autonomy

Digital identities can also infringe on individuals' personal freedom and autonomy. Digital identities can be used to track individuals' online activity and behavior, monitor their location, and limit their access to certain services or resources. This can result in individuals being subjected to invasive surveillance and other negative consequences that limit their personal freedom and autonomy.

4. Inequality and Discrimination

Digital identities can also lead to inequality and discrimination, particularly for individuals from marginalized communities. Digital identities may not be available to all individuals, either due to a lack of access to digital infrastructure or other barriers. Additionally, digital identities can be used to discriminate against individuals based on factors such as race, gender, or sexual orientation. This can have significant negative impacts on individuals' access to opportunities, services, and resources.

The Benefits of Digital Identities

1. Convenience and Access to Services

Digital identities offer a high degree of convenience and access to services. Digital identities enable individuals to access a wide range of online services, such as online shopping, online banking, and e-government services. This can save time and effort for individuals, as they do not need to physically visit a location to access these services.

2. Increased Security

Digital identities can also offer increased security. With the use of digital identities, individuals can secure their personal data with multi-factor authentication and encryption. This can prevent unauthorized access to personal data, protecting individuals from identity theft and fraud.

3. Improved Efficiency

Digital identities can improve the efficiency of many processes, such as identity verification and authentication. With digital identities, individuals can quickly and easily prove their identity, without the need for physical identification documents. This can lead to faster processing times and reduced administrative burdens.

4. Improved Financial Inclusion

Digital identities can also contribute to improved financial inclusion. Digital identities enable individuals to access financial services, such as bank accounts and loans, without the need for physical identification documents. This can benefit individuals who are underbanked or unbanked, enabling them to access financial services and participate in the formal economy.

Mitigating the Risk of Digital Identities

Introduce data protection laws and regulations that require organizations to take steps to protect personal data. These laws and regulations can require organizations to obtain individuals' consent before collecting and using their data, implement robust data security measures, and notify individuals in the event of a data breach. These measures can help protect individuals' personal data and reduce the risk of identity theft and fraud.

Education and AwarenessIndividuals can also take steps to protect their digital identities by educating themselves about the risks and taking appropriate measures. This includes using strong and unique passwords, enabling two-factor authentication, avoiding sharing personal information online, and being vigilant for phishing scams and other forms of social engineering.

Decentralized identity solutions offer an alternative to traditional digital identities that are controlled by centralized organizations. Decentralized identity solutions use blockchain technology to store and manage individuals' identity data, enabling individuals to have more control over their personal data and reducing the risk of data breaches and other forms of abuse.

Privacy by design is an approach to designing products and services that takes into account privacy and data protection from the outset. This involves incorporating privacy and data protection principles into the design and development process, such as minimizing data collection and retention, using strong encryption and data security measures, and enabling individuals to control their personal data.

Conclusion

Digital identities offer numerous benefits, including convenience, improved security, and increased efficiency. However, they also pose significant risks to individual privacy and security, including identity theft, privacy breaches, and infringement of personal freedom and autonomy. To mitigate these risks, a range of measures can be taken, including data protection laws and regulations, education and awareness, decentralized identity solutions, and privacy by design. By implementing these measures, we can harness the benefits of digital identities while protecting individuals' privacy and security

Chapter 4: The Dark Side of the Intersection of 15 Minute Cities, Central Bank Digital Currencies, and Digital Identities

The advent of 15 minute cities has promised a world where everything is accessible within a short walk or bike ride. This will be made possible by the widespread adoption of central bank digital currencies (CBDCs) and digital identities. The idea is that these technologies will make transactions easier, faster, and more secure. However, this utopian vision has a dark side that few have anticipated.

The convergence of 15 minute cities, CBDCs, and digital identities has created a powerful tool for controlling people's lives. Governments and corporations will have unprecedented access to people's personal data, spending habits, and even their movements. This gives them the power to track, monitor, and manipulate people's behavior in ways that were previously unimaginable.

One of the most concerning aspects of this new system is the potential for abuse. Governments and corporations could use people's data to target them with advertisements, influence their political views, and even deny them access to certain services based on their behavior. For example, if someone was deemed to be a risk to society, they could be denied access to public transportation, healthcare, or even employment.

Another issue was the potential for data breaches. With so much personal data being stored in centralized databases, the risk of a cyber attack is significant. If a malicious actor gained access to these databases, they would have access to people's personal information, financial records, and even their location data. This would be a disaster for individuals, and could also have far-reaching consequences for society as a whole.

There is also the potential for the system to be abused by those in power. Governments could use people's data to track dissidents and suppress dissent. This has already been happening in some countries, where activists were being monitored and punished for their activities. Similarly, corporations could use people's data to manipulate them into buying products they didn't need or even to sway their political views.

Another issue is the potential for discrimination. With so much data being collected on people's behavior, there is a risk that certain groups could be unfairly targeted. For example, if a certain group was found to be more likely to engage in criminal activity, they could be discriminated against when it came to access to services or employment. This would be a gross violation of their rights and could lead to social unrest.

Perhaps the most concerning aspect of this system is the potential for totalitarianism. With so much power in the hands of so few, there is a risk that governments could become tyrannical. They could use people's data to monitor and control their behavior, creating a society where dissent is not tolerated and freedom of speech is a thing of the past. This would be a dystopian nightmare, and would be a major step back for human rights and democracy.

In conclusion, the intersection of 15 minute cities, CBDCs, and digital identities has the potential to be both a blessing and a curse. While these technologies have the potential to make life easier and more convenient, they also have the potential to be used for nefarious purposes. Governments and corporations had unprecedented access to people's personal data, and this could be used to track, monitor, and manipulate people's behavior. The potential for abuse is significant, and there is a risk of data breaches, discrimination, and even totalitarianism. It is important that these issues are addressed before this new system becomes the norm, and that individuals' rights and freedoms are protected.

Chapter 5: Conclusion: Navigating the Future of Urbanism

The future of urbanism is an exciting yet daunting prospect. With the rise of new technologies, the way we interact with our cities is changing rapidly. In this book, we have explored the potential of 15 minute cities, central bank digital currencies, and digital identities and their intersection, as well as the potential risks and unintended consequences that come with them. In this final chapter, we will summarize our findings and offer recommendations for navigating the future of urbanism.

15 Minute Cities: A Sustainable and Livable Future?

The concept of 15 minute cities is a promising vision of a more sustainable and livable future. By creating cities where everything is accessible within a 15-minute walk or bike ride, we can reduce our reliance on cars, promote healthier lifestyles, and create more vibrant and connected communities. However, as we discussed in chapter 1, there are challenges to implementing this vision. Land use policies, zoning regulations, and transportation infrastructure all need to be aligned to create a 15 minute city. In addition, we need to ensure that these cities are inclusive and equitable, and that all members of society have access to the services and amenities they need.

Central Bank Digital Currencies: A New Era of Transactions?

Central bank digital currencies have the potential to revolutionize the way we transact. As we discussed in chapter 2, CBDCs offer many benefits over traditional fiat currencies, including faster and more secure transactions, reduced costs, and increased financial inclusion. However, there are also risks associated with CBDCs. For example, if they are not designed properly, they could exacerbate existing economic inequalities or pose a risk to financial stability. It is important that policymakers carefully consider the design and implementation of CBDCs to ensure that they promote economic growth, financial stability, and social welfare.

Digital Identities: A New Era of Personal Data?

Digital identities are becoming an increasingly important aspect of our lives. As we discussed in chapter 3, they offer many benefits, including increased security, convenience, and personalization. However, there are also risks associated with digital identities, particularly in the context of privacy and security. Governments and corporations have unprecedented access to people's personal data, and there is a risk that this data could be used for nefarious purposes. It is important that individuals have control over their own data and that privacy and security protections are built into the design of digital identity systems.

The Dark Side of the Intersection

The intersection of 15 minute cities, CBDCs, and digital identities has the potential to create a powerful tool for controlling people's lives. As we discussed in chapter 4, this system could be used to track, monitor, and manipulate people's behavior in ways that are unprecedented. Governments and corporations could use people's data to target them with advertisements, influence their political views, and even deny them access to certain services based on their behavior. There is also the potential for discrimination, data breaches, and even totalitarianism. It is important that these risks are carefully considered and addressed before this new system becomes the norm.

Recommendations

In order to navigate the future of urbanism, we must carefully consider the potential benefits and risks of new technologies. We offer the following recommendations for policymakers, urban planners, and designers:

1. Prioritize inclusivity and equity in the design of 15 minute cities. Ensure that all members of society have access to the services and amenities they need.
2. Ensure that CBDCs are designed in a way that promotes economic growth, financial stability, and social welfare, while also addressing potential risks.
3. Build privacy and security protections into the design of digital identity systems. Ensure that individuals have control over their own data and that data breaches are minimized.
4. Address the potential risks of the intersection of 15 minute cities, CBDCs, and

digital identities, including the potential for surveillance, discrimination, and totalitarianism.

5. Encourage public debate and engagement on the use of new technologies in urbanism. Ensure that all stakeholders, including citizens, are informed and have a say in the decisions that affect their lives.

6. Invest in research and development to understand the potential benefits and risks of new technologies in urbanism. This will help policymakers and designers make informed decisions about how to use these technologies.

7. Foster collaboration and cooperation between different sectors and stakeholders. The future of urbanism requires a holistic and collaborative approach, with governments, businesses, and communities working together to create sustainable and livable cities.

Conclusion

The future of urbanism is full of promise and potential, but it also comes with risks and challenges. The intersection of 15 minute cities, CBDCs, and digital identities offers many benefits, but it also has the potential to harm citizens if not designed and implemented properly. As we navigate this new era of urbanism, it is important that we prioritize inclusivity, equity, privacy, and security, and that we engage in public debate and collaboration to ensure that these new technologies are used for the benefit of society as a whole. By doing so, we can create a sustainable and livable future for all.

Printed in Great Britain
by Amazon

23759001R00030